W9-BYI-083

A Great Idea

Becoming Invisible:
From Camouflage to Cloaks

by Carla Mooney

NORWOOD HOUSE PRESS

Cover: A camouflaged soldier and his gun, left, are barely visible in his hiding place. A woman's invisibility cloak makes it appear that people can see right through her. A fish, scarcely visible in the water, right, is an example of Nature's camouflage.

Norwood House Press
P.O. Box 316598
Chicago, Illinois 60631

For information regarding Norwood House Press, please visit our Web site at:

www.norwoodhousepress.com or call 866-565-2900.

PHOTO CREDITS: Cover photos: U.S. Navy photo (left); AP Images (center); CC-By-SA-2.5/Moondigger/Wikipedia (right); AP Images, 10, 12, 21, 30; Bow Publications, 27; BSIP/Photo Researchers, Inc., 28; Courtesy Edit International, 39; Val Gempis/UPI/Landov, 20; Getty Images, 36; Hulton Archive/Getty Images, 5, 8, 9; Chris Ison/PA Photos/Landov, 14; Photofest NYC, 4, 23; Courtesy Physicsworld .com, 42; Reuters/Landov, 31; Courtesy of Tachilabs, 38; Universal/The Kobal Collection/The Picture Desk, 24; Courtesy University of California, Berkeley, 41; UPI Photo/U.S. Air Force/Landov, 18; Art Wolfe/ Photo Researchers, Inc., 29; © WorldFoto/Alamy, 6; Steve Zmina, 13, 17, 33, 37

© 2011 by Norwood House Press.

All rights reserved.

No part of this book may be reproduced without written permission from the publisher.

LIBRARY OF CONGRESS CATALOGING-IN-PUBLICATION DATA

Mooney, Carla, 1970–
  Becoming invisible : from camouflage to cloaks / Carla Mooney.
    p. cm. — (A great idea)
  Includes bibliographical references and index.
  Summary: "Throughout history, from the art of camouflage to the science of stealth technology, ways have been developed to hide objects and people. Today, scientists are building an "invisibility cloak" that makes objects and people underneath it seem to disappear"—Provided by publisher.
  ISBN-13: 978-1-59953-378-0 (library edition: alk. paper)
  ISBN-10: 1-59953-378-2 (library edition: alk. paper)
  1. Camouflage (Military science)—Juvenile literature. 2. Optical engineering—Juvenile literature. 3. Optical materials—Juvenile literature. 4. Visibility—Juvenile literature. 5. Disappearances (Parapsychology)—Juvenile literature. I. Title.
  UG449.M66 2010
  623'.77—dc22
                                                2010016516

Manufactured in the United States of America in North Mankato, Minnesota.
164N—072010

Contents

Note: Words that are **bolded** in the text are defined in the glossary on page 44.

Chapter 1

The World's Best Camouflage

Harry Potter is a world-famous fictional wizard. When he was eleven years old, he received a mysterious gift. As he unwrapped the package, Harry discovered an old cloak. When he put the cloak on, however, Harry realized that it was much more than an ordinary piece of cloth. The cloak made his body disappear! Harry's present was a rare invisibility cloak. He would use it many times to become invisible during his adventures at the Hogwarts wizard school.

His body covered by an invisibility cloak, Harry Potter's head seems to float in thin air.

Harry Potter's invisibility cloak sparked the imagination of readers and moviegoers around the world. What if people could simply slip on a cloak and disappear? Someday such a cloak may become real. Scientists are already working on ways to make objects invisible.

Searching for Invisibility

Humans have always searched for ways to be less visible. People who depend on **stealth** could do their jobs better if they went unnoticed. Spies could watch targets unseen. Hunters could stalk prey without scaring them away. Researchers

In 18th-century Wyoming, Native American hunters use animal skins for camouflage as they creep up on a herd of bison.

could study animals without disturbing them.

For the military, being able to make troops and weapons invisible would be an incredible advantage. If soldiers can be seen, they can be shot. If enemy troops could not see the soldiers, they would not know where to aim their weapons. Armies could move soldiers secretly. Once they were in place, the invisible soldiers could suddenly appear. The enemy troops would not know that they were surrounded until it was too late.

Hidden by Camouflage

Until recently, the power of invisibility could be achieved only in movies and fiction. However, the development of camouflage came close to creating invisibility. Camouflage is a way of disguising an object. A camouflaged object blends into its background.

Spots on an African leopard's body make him harder to see as he hides in tall grass.

The idea of camouflage came from animals. In the late 1800s, artist Abbott Thayer studied animals. He was fascinated by their markings and colors. Thayer realized that many animals had colors and marks that made them harder to see in the wild. A zebra's stripes allowed it to blend into the shadows of the grasslands. A leopard's spots hid it in the dappled shade of the trees so it was better able to pounce from above on its prey.

Thayer thought that humans could also use color and markings to hide. During the Spanish-American War, he suggested that the navy paint its ships with special camouflage patterns. The war ended before Thayer's idea could be used. Still, the idea of camouflage began to spread.

Did You Know?

In Greek mythology the goddess Athena wore an invisibility cap during the Trojan War. She wanted to be invisible to Ares, the god of war, when she helped warriors during the battles.

During World War I, many countries had tested camouflage on land, sea, and air. They worked with artists and nature experts to create camouflage patterns. Each country created its own designs with muted colors such as gray, brown, and green. Some uniforms had patterns of colored dots all over them. Others used jagged stripes across the uniform. All of the patterns helped soldiers blend into the background better. Before long, scientists

Marine Dazzle Camouflage

During World War I, the U.S. military developed camouflage called "dazzle" for ships. Dazzle camouflage was a random pattern of stripes, swirls, and zigzags. It often looked like a giant cubist painting. Cubism was an abstract art style that began in the early 20th century. Painters like Pablo Picasso created pictures using a combination of **geometric** shapes.

One ship painted with dazzle camouflage was the SS *Massachusetts*, an 8,000-ton (7,258-metric-ton) freighter. On the bridge the crew painted a combination of black, blue, white, and grayish-green shapes. On the hull they painted curves and zigzags. Researchers believe these patterns were not meant to hide the ship. Instead these dazzle camouflage patterns were supposed to confuse the enemy. Different patterns on different parts of a ship made it harder for the enemy to see important areas of the ship. It also made it harder for enemy gunners to figure out the ship's speed, direction, and distance.

A World War I ship is painted in dazzle camouflage.

also began to design camouflage. They studied how the human eye finds and sees an object. Then they created complex patterns to trick the eye.

In World War II, military leaders used camouflage to hide valuable objects and buildings. They hid airports, oil tankers, and factories from enemy planes. Troops used nets, branches, and smoke to hide these objects.

Today the military has camouflage to help it hide in every type of **terrain**. Some camouflage patterns use greens and browns to hide soldiers in forests. Sand-colored patterns work in desert regions. In addition, the military

A soldier blends into his surroundings in this rare color photo of World War II camouflage.

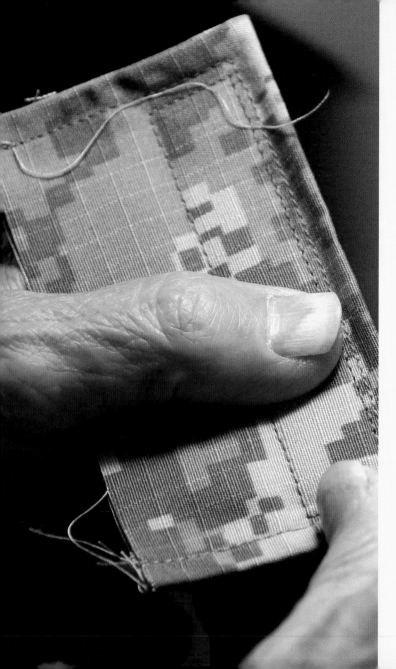

uses digital technology to create camouflage patterns. Up close, the digital pattern has small blocks that look like pixels from a video screen. The colors blend smoothly, without a hard line between them. In addition, the pixels make the uniform look as if it has **texture**. From a distance, the texture and smoothly blended colors help the digital pattern blend into the background better. This makes a soldier harder to see. A soldier in a digital camouflage uniform is 40 percent less likely to be seen than a soldier in a traditional uniform is. The military also has camouflage that can be painted on tanks. There are even vinyl wraps that match the surrounding

This example of digital camouflage shows the pattern of colored blocks used in soldiers' uniforms.

Making a City Disappear

During World War II, British prime minister Winston Churchill feared that the Germans were preparing to bomb the valuable port of Alexandria in Egypt. Churchill turned to professional magician Jasper Maskelyne for help. He asked Maskelyne to make the African port invisible from the sky. Maskelyne's unit was called the Magic Gang. It included set designers, painters, and architects. During the night, the Magic Gang built a fake harbor 3 miles (4.8km) away from Alexandria. They turned out all the lights in the real city. Then they turned out most of the lights in the fake city but allowed a few to shine. From the air the German bombers saw the few lights from the fake city and thought it was their target. They dropped their bombs on the fake city. The real city of Alexandria was saved.

land. These wraps make a truck, plane, or weapon look like its background.

People and tanks wearing camouflage may be harder to see, but they are not invisible. They can still be discovered. Scientists have dreamed of solving this problem with an invisibility cloak. Anyone wearing the cloak would be invisible.

Optical Camouflage

Dr. Susumu Tachi is a researcher at the University of Tokyo. He wanted to create an invisibility cloak. In 2003 he tested an invisibility cloak that worked with **optical** camouflage. Optical camouflage uses cameras, projectors, and other equipment. It projects a picture of the background

A woman wears optical camouflage, which makes it appear that we can see right through her!

scene onto an object. This creates the illusion of invisibility.

To make his cloak work, Tachi set up a camera and a projector. He placed a person wearing a special cloak in front of the projector. The cloak looked like a large raincoat. It was made of thousands of small, highly reflective beads. A video camera filmed the scene behind the person. Then a projector played the computer-processed video on the cloak. A viewer standing directly in front of the cloaked person saw the background video on the cloak. It looked as if the viewer could see through the cloak to the scene behind it. The parts of the body covered by the cloak seemed to disappear.

Did You Know?

The word *camouflage* comes from the French word *camoufler,* which means "to conceal or cover up."

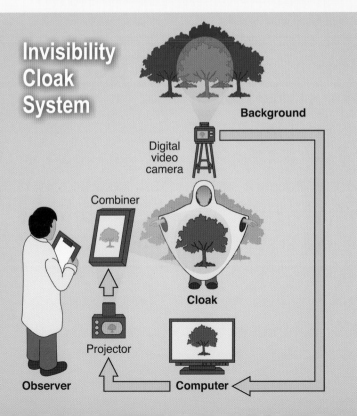

Invisibility Cloak System

Background

Digital video camera

Combiner

Cloak

Projector

Observer

Computer

Making a Tank Disappear

In October 2007, the British military tested optical camouflage on a tank. Military officials and scientists gathered at an isolated military base in southern England. Across the field a British Challenger tank rumbled into view. The tank weighed 60 tons (54.4 metric tons) and was about 30 feet (9.1m) long. It was the size of a small house. As the viewers watched, the tank simply vanished. They could see only an empty field. In reality, the powerful tank still faced them. It had become invisible.

Instead of using a cloak like Tachi's, the British researchers had coated the tank with **silicone**. This made it like a highly reflective movie screen. Then video cameras on the tank took pictures of the field around the tank. The researchers projected

In 2007, the British military covered a Challenger tank like this one with silicone, making it "invisible."

the video onto the tank itself. To those watching, the tank blended into the field and seemed to disappear.

The First Step to Invisibility

Optical camouflage can make a person's body or a tank seem to disappear. Still, scientists believe it is only the first step on the journey toward building a working invisibility cloak. Right now optical camouflage works from only one angle. If the viewer moves to the side, he or she can no longer see the projected image. It is like moving to the side of a flat-screen television or movie screen and not being able to see the show anymore. From the side the viewer would be able to see the object being hidden. In addition, optical camouflage uses a lot of equipment to make an object disappear. This equipment has to be set up exactly

Hiding in Plain Sight

In ancient Japan, Ninja fighters figured out how to become invisible without really disappearing. They learned how to hide in plain sight. The human eye normally has a field of vision of about 60 degrees when looking straight ahead. The eye can see up to 100 degrees with peripheral (side) vision. When a person focuses on an object, the brain shrinks the field of vision. It may narrow to as little as 6 degrees. The person becomes blind to the rest of his or her surroundings. Ninjas learned how to take advantage of this blind spot. They hid unseen in the shadows until a person focused his or her gaze on another object. Then they attacked during the split second the person had a blind spot. Their targets never saw them coming.

Did You Know?

The goldenrod spider can change its color from white to yellow to camouflage itself in flowers.

right. If one piece is out of place, the optical camouflage does not work.

Scientists are working to solve these problems and make a better invisibility cloak. A true cloak would need to work from all angles. It would also need to work without a lot of complicated equipment. Then perhaps a person wearing an invisibility cloak would be able to move and walk unseen, just like Harry Potter tiptoeing through the halls of Hogwarts. In the meantime, people are using different types of camouflage to hide objects today.

Chapter 2

How Invisibility Works Today

The science to make something truly invisible is still in the early stages. A working invisibility cloak may be years away. In the meantime people are making objects seem invisible today using other technology.

Stealth Technology

Some airplanes use stealth technology to fly without being detected. These planes are not invisible. The human eye can see them. Instead, they are invisible to radar.

Radar works like visible light. First, a radar antenna sends out a burst of radio energy. When the radio waves hit an object, they reflect back to the antenna. The antenna measures how long it takes the reflection to return. This tells it how far away the object is. Waves returning from a close object will return sooner than waves bouncing off an object farther away. The radar equipment also uses the reflected waves to track where the object moves.

Many countries use radar systems to track planes that fly over their land. The metal bodies of airplanes reflect radar signals well. In addition, most planes have a rounded shape. The curves make planes **aerodynamic**. They also reflect radar waves in many directions. This makes it easy for some of the radar waves to bounce back to the radar antenna. Radar systems can then easily find and track airplanes. When flying over enemy land, however, pilots may not want their planes to be seen. They can spy on an enemy better if they are invisible. Flying unseen also keeps planes and pilots safer from enemy fire.

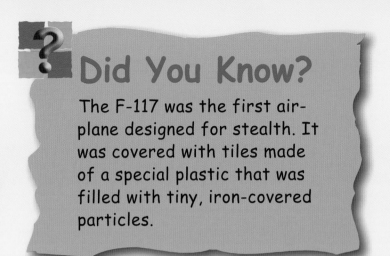

Did You Know?

The F-117 was the first airplane designed for stealth. It was covered with tiles made of a special plastic that was filled with tiny, iron-covered particles.

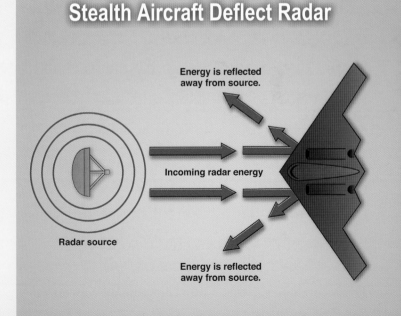

Stealth Aircraft Deflect Radar

Energy is reflected away from source.

Incoming radar energy

Radar source

Energy is reflected away from source.

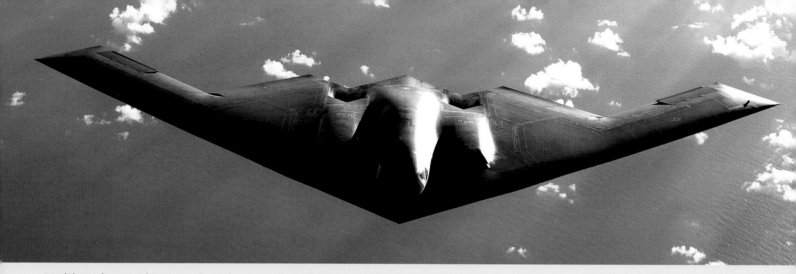

Unlike planes designed with a rounded shape, which can easily be tracked by radar, the B-2 stealth aircraft's flat shape is specially designed to fool enemy radar.

One way to make a plane invisible to radar is to change its shape. Instead of a rounded shape, stealth planes have flat surfaces and sharp edges. A flat surface usually reflects energy in only one direction. When a radar signal hits a stealth plane, the wave reflects at a **perpendicular** angle. It will only reflect back to the radar antenna if the plane is directly over or under the radar source.

A stealth aircraft also uses special materials and coatings to disguise it from radar. These do not make the plane completely invisible. Instead they absorb radar waves and reduce reflection. Sending back fewer reflected waves makes the aircraft appear smaller on radar. A stealth plane may look as if it is a small bird on a radar screen.

The B-2 bomber is one type of stealth aircraft. Crews construct the bomber from a combination of lightweight materials that absorb radio waves. Some parts cannot be made from radar-absorbing materials. Instead flight crews cover them with radar-absorbing paint or tape. After each flight, the repair crew examines the plane. They make sure all parts are still covered with radar-absorbing material. One small gap can cause the plane to reflect radar beams to an enemy's radar antenna.

Stealth technology lowers the chance that a plane will be detected by radar. It cannot make a plane disappear. Before a mission, ground crews spend hours working on a stealth plane. They make sure that all of the plane's seams are even. If

The Hopeless Diamond

In the 1970s engineers at Lockheed Corporation studied ways to make a stealth airplane. They built a 10-foot (3m) wooden model plane. The model plane looked like a squat diamond with sharp edges and flat surfaces. Some thought it looked too hopeless to fly. This inspired the model's name, the Hopeless Diamond. To test it, engineers placed the model on a pole and directed radar waves at it. The model plane reflected the radar waves away from the receiver. The radar operator was unable to "see" the model. The successful test made engineers think that it might be possible one day to create an airplane that would be "invisible" to radar.

they find a rough spot, they smooth it so that it will not reflect a radar wave. They cover the seams with radar-absorbing tape. The crew also paints the plane with

After a mission, airmen at a New Mexico air force base check a stealth bomber to make sure that all radar-absorbing materials have not been damaged.

radar-absorbing materials. Still, none of their efforts can make the plane truly disappear. Before a mission, pilots and crews carefully plan their flight path. They try to avoid all known enemy radar sites. If the plane flies directly over a hidden radar site, it will be discovered.

Blue-Screen Backgrounds

Television studios also use a type of invisibility. Anyone who has watched a weather reporter in front of a map has seen this technology in action. In the studio the reporter stands in front of a solid blue or green screen. The reporter points to it as if he or she can see objects on the screen. When the video broadcasts on television, the colored screen disappears. Instead viewers see a weather map.

Green-screen or blue-screen backgrounds are often used to create special effects in filming movies and TV programs, such as *Battlestar Galactica*, right.

News crews use cameras and computers to make the blue screen disappear. First, cameras film the reporter in front of the screen. Then computers remove the solid background from the video. They replace it with another video clip or **animation**. For weather reports, the computer places maps and graphics behind the reporter.

When filming with a blue screen, the reporter cannot wear the background color. If he or she wears a blue shirt by accident, the computer will erase and replace the shirt along with the blue background. The person would look as if he or she had a floating head and hands.

? Did You Know?

Any solid color will work with blue-screen technology. Blue and green are the most popular choices because they are the colors least like a person's skin tone.

Movie Magic

Blue-screen technology can also make people and objects disappear on film. In *Harry Potter and the Sorcerer's Stone*, Harry disappears under an old cloak. To create this on-screen magic, filmmakers used a version of blue-screen technology. Movie directors also use blue screens to replace backgrounds. Action stars appear to dangle over cliffs. Superman flies through the sky. Some movies and television shows replace an entire city background. This makes it look as if the actors are walking down a Paris street when they have never left Los Angeles!

Creating the Invisible Man

In the 1992 movie *Memoirs of an Invisible Man,* filmmakers had to make actor Chevy Chase disappear. In one scene, Chase stripped off his shirt while running from villains. Filmmakers had to make it look like his empty pants were running. They had Chase wear a hooded blue bodysuit under his clothes. When he took off his shirt, they filmed him running in the blue bodysuit and regular pants. After filming, a computer removed Chase's blue-covered upper body and head from the scene, so his pants appeared to be running without a body. An artist added a photograph of an empty pair of pants to the computer image. The artist then matched the waistband of the empty pants to the running pants and pasted it onto the computer image. He had created an invisible man.

Movie magic can also make one part of an actor disappear. In the movie *Percy Jackson and the Olympians: The Lightning Thief*, actor Pierce Brosnan's character is a centaur. This means his character has a human upper body. His lower half is a horse's body and legs. To make Brosnan's actual legs disappear, he wore blue tights when he filmed his scenes. The crew then used computers to erase his legs on the film. They replaced them with a digital image of a horse's body and legs. To viewers Brosnan's character appears to be half horse and half human.

In the movie *Forrest Gump*, actor Gary Sinise also needed to appear without legs. He played a veteran who had lost his legs in the Vietnam War. To create this illusion, the film crew wrapped Sinise's legs in blue fabric. Computers removed the legs. On-screen, Sinise's legless body looked incredibly real.

Computer "magic" used in the movie *Forrest Gump* made it appear that actor Gary Sinise's character had lost his legs.

The Next Step to Invisibility

Today people are using camouflage, stealth technology, and blue screens to hide objects. At the same time, scientists are working on the next step toward building a working invisibility cloak. They believe the key to invisibility lies in changing how light behaves.

Humans use light to see. A person staring at a coffee cup does not actually see

Invisibility in Fiction

Humans have written books and made movies about invisibility for years. Some memorable examples include:

- In 1897 H.G. Wells published his novel *The Invisible Man*. His main character uses bleach and mysterious rays to make himself disappear.
- In 1937 J.R.R. Tolkien created his fantasy novel *The Hobbit*. The book's main character, Bilbo Baggins, discovers a gold ring that makes its wearer invisible.
- In the television show *Star Trek,* the Romulans use a cloaking device to hide their spaceship and surprise the crew of the USS *Enterprise* in an episode that aired in 1966.

A poster for the 1933 movie of H.G. Wells's book *The Invisible Man.*

Did You Know?

Germany painted submarine periscopes with radar-absorbing materials during World War II so that the periscopes could rise above water without being "seen."

the cup. Instead he or she sees light waves that bounce off the cup. The bounced light waves return to the eye. They form a reflection that enters the eye. The reflection creates an image of the cup on the eye's retina. The person now sees the cup. Without light bouncing back to the eye, the person would not be able to see the cup. For example, if the room were completely dark, it would be very difficult to see anything.

To make an object invisible, scientists would need to build something that does not reflect waves of light. They would have to find a way to make light bend around an object instead of reflecting back into the viewer's eyes. This would be like playing a trick on the eye by **manipulating** light. The invisible object would not really disappear. Changing how light behaves would fool the eye into thinking the object is no longer there. Then the object would seem to be invisible.

Chapter 3

Researching Invisibility Cloaks

D r. David Smith is a professor of physics and engineering at Duke University. He and his team of researchers are working on ways to bend and control light. Smith believes that manipulating light is the key to building a true invisibility cloak.

Light Is Everywhere

First, Smith's team studied light and how it behaves. Light is a type of radiation. It travels in waves through space like water waves travel through the ocean. Like ocean waves, light waves have high points called crests and low points called troughs. Radiation waves are made up of electric and magnetic fields. Each type of light wave has a different wavelength and frequency. Wavelength is the distance from one crest to the next. Frequency is the number of waves that travel by a fixed spot in one second. Waves that are more spread out have longer wavelengths and lower frequencies.

The light that humans see is called visible light. It has short wavelengths and high frequencies. Together, all types of radiation waves are called the **electromagnetic** spectrum.

Reflection and Refraction

When light hits an object, some of it bounces off and reflects. In addition, some light waves pass through the object. When a light wave passes through an object, it bends, or refracts. This happens because the light wave changes speed

The Color of Light

Visible light is made of several colors. Each color has a different wavelength. Red is the longest, and violet is the shortest. In order from long to short, the colors are red, orange, yellow, green, blue, indigo, and violet. This is also the order of colors in a rainbow. Many people use the letters "ROY G BIV" to remember the order of light's colors. The colors of light refract at different angles. That is why light passing through a prism separates into a rainbow. A working invisibility cloak would have to control each of these colors and their different wavelengths.

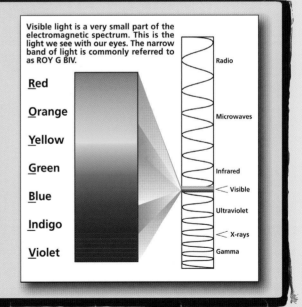

Visible light is a very small part of the electromagnetic spectrum. This is the light we see with our eyes. The narrow band of light is commonly referred to as ROY G BIV.

Red
Orange
Yellow
Green
Blue
Indigo
Violet

Radio
Microwaves
Infrared
Visible
Ultraviolet
X-rays
Gamma

? Did You Know?

Refraction of light causes **mirages**, rainbows, and the colors of the sunrise and sunset.

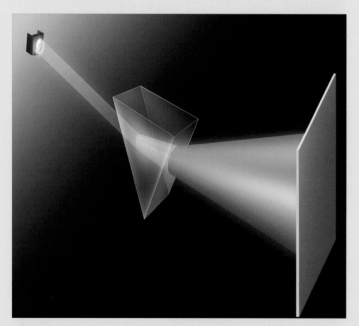

In this illustration, white light, left, passing through a prism breaks into all the colors of the spectrum.

when it moves through objects with different **densities**. If the object is denser, the light travels more slowly through it. If the object is less dense, light waves travel faster through it.

For example, when a light wave moves from the air through a piece of glass, which is denser, it slows down. The light wave bends where the two materials—air and glass—meet. This bending is called refraction. In the glass example, the wave front bends because it is moving more slowly than the rest of the wave. Light does not refract randomly. It always bends the same way in the same material.

Controlling Light

To make an object invisible, Smith's team needed to change how it reflects and refracts light. Light would have to flow smoothly around an object instead of reflecting and refracting. When it reached the other side, the light waves would have to flow as if they had never been disturbed. Without a reflection reaching the eye, a person would see nothing. It would be like water flowing around a rock in a stream. The water flows smoothly around the rock. Downstream, the water returns to its normal flow pattern. Looking at the water downstream, a person could not tell that it had been disturbed upstream earlier by the rock.

To control light around an object in this way, Smith's team would have to change the way light bends. For years scientists thought this was impossible. Light always behaved in the same way with

Dr. Smith wanted to make light waves flow around objects in the same way that water flows around this large rock.

natural materials. Then British researcher John Pendry developed a new theory. He thought it was possible to control how light bends around objects using tiny, human-made materials called metamaterials. Smith read Pendry's paper about metamaterials. He thought he could use them to control light.

Metamaterials

Metamaterials are a combination of materials that can control the way light bends. They are often made of simple materials like metal and fiberglass. Each of these simple materials cannot control light by itself. Together in a metamaterial, however, they can. Their size and shape and the combination of the materials with each other give them magnetic and elec-

Researchers have discovered that metamaterials like the one above are useful in making objects seem to disappear.

trical properties. These properties give metamaterials the ability to control how light bends. This allows them to make light flow around an object. There is little reflection, which makes an object appear as if it is not there.

To make a metamaterial, researchers design rows and columns of tiny structures. These structures can be coils, loops, antennas, or holes. The structures can be cut into the surface of a circuit board. They can also be layered like a computer chip. Scientists cut and arrange them in a way that bends light waves in a specific direction. The size, shape, and position of each structure affect how it interacts with light.

Metamaterials are hard to make. Their tiny components must be smaller than light's wavelength.

A microscopic view of a metamaterial shows how precisely these special materials must be designed. Each layer fits perfectly with the next.

? Did You Know?

Part of the word *metamaterials* comes from the Greek word *meta,* which means "beyond."

Wavelengths of visible light are only **nanometers** in length. It would take more than 100 visible light wavelengths placed end to end to equal the width of a human hair. Metamaterials must also be designed exactly right in order to guide light in a controlled way.

Making a Cloak with Metamaterials

Building an invisibility cloak with metamaterials is an enormous task. Scientists line up thousands of tiny structures in rows on a cloak. These structures pick up a ray of light on one side of an object. Then the devices send that ray around the object, row by row. When the light reaches the other side of the object, the structures re-form the light as if nothing had been in its way. For the cloak to work best, it would have to bend light coming in from all directions.

Testing a Metamaterial Cloak with Microwaves

In 2006 Smith tested a new invisibility cloak. He used metamaterials to build the cloak. Smith made the cloak from narrow bands of fiberglass. He placed a thin layer of copper on top of each band. Then he imprinted thousands of tiny circles and

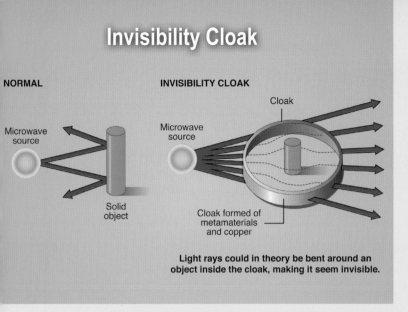

Invisibility Cloak

NORMAL

Microwave source

Solid object

INVISIBILITY CLOAK

Cloak

Microwave source

Cloak formed of metamaterials and copper

Light rays could in theory be bent around an object inside the cloak, making it seem invisible.

materials must be shorter than the light waves that they are going to bend. Microwaves are millimeters long. Therefore, the metamaterials Smith used would also be millimeters in length. Working with shorter waves, such as visible light, would be much harder. Since visible light is only nanometers in length, the metamaterials would also need to be nanometers small.

Smith used a microwave-based radar machine to see what happened when the microwaves hit his cloak. When microwaves hit an object, they normally reflect and scatter. When they hit Smith's cloaked object, the tiny metal circles and rods changed the directions of the electric and magnetic fields of the waves. This allowed the cloak to move the waves around

rods on each band. Smith formed the bands into circles and nested them inside each other. The device was small, about 5 inches (12.7cm) wide. At the center Smith placed a small object.

Then Smith directed **microwaves** at the cloaked object. Smith chose to work with microwaves because they are one of the longest light waves. To work, meta-

itself. Then the waves re-formed on the other side of the object. It appeared as if the waves had not been disturbed. The object was invisible to the microwaves.

Smith's cloak did not make objects invisible to the human eye. It did, however, show that it was possible to bend and control light waves. If scientists could make Smith's method work with visible light, they could create a true invisibility cloak.

Moving Closer to Visible Light

In 2008 researcher Xiang Zhang moved a step closer to controlling visible light. He made a metamaterial that worked with **infrared** light. Infrared light is shorter than microwaves but longer than vis-

Blind Inside

There is still one major drawback to wearing an invisibility cloak. The person wearing the cloak is not able to see. The human eye uses light to see. The cloak's materials reflect light around the cloak. As a result, very little light penetrates the cloak. This means there is not enough light for the eye to see. To make a cloak for humans, scientists will have to figure out a way to see from inside the cloak. Otherwise, the invisible person may walk into a wall!

ible light. First, Zhang alternated sheets of silver and **magnesium fluoride**. Then he drilled a fishnet pattern of rectangular holes in the stacked sheets. The metamaterial acted like an opposing magnet. It pushed on the incoming light and bent it around the cloaked object. The object became invisible in infrared light.

Zhang says that changing the size of the holes will allow researchers to work with different-sized light wavelengths. He thinks that if the fishnet metamaterial could be made smaller, it would work with visible light. Then the fishnet metamaterial could be used to make objects invisible to the human eye.

Carpet Cloaks

In their early research, both Smith and Zhang used metallic metamaterials. Using metals, however, did have a drawback. Metal absorbs a lot of light. If the material absorbs too much light, not enough light moves around the cloaked object and re-forms on the other side. A material that does not absorb light would be able to send most of the light waves around the cloaked object. This would do a better job of making an object disappear.

In 2009 Zhang and other researchers created a **silicon** metamaterial. They used it to make a carpetlike invisibility cloak. Zhang's lab at the University of California at Berkeley drilled **nanoscale** holes into a piece of silicon. The silicon was only 250 nanometers thick. Each

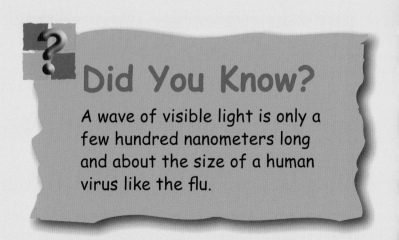

Did You Know?

A wave of visible light is only a few hundred nanometers long and about the size of a human virus like the flu.

drilled hole was only 110 nanometers wide. The holes transformed the silicon slab into a metamaterial. The silicon metamaterial absorbed less light than previous metal ones. Most of the light now flowed around the slab.

Zhang's team used the carpet cloak to hide a bump on a thin layer of material. The bump was the size and shape of a child hiding under a blanket. Shining an infrared light on the side of the bump normally casts a shadow. Under

Nanotechnology

Nanotechnology is the study of objects so small that even a light microscope cannot see them. A nanometer is one-billionth of a meter. It is about one-hundred-thousandth the width of a human hair. The head of a pin is about one million nanometers. To study objects so small, scientists use special microscopes. These microscopes scan nano-size objects and send the data to a computer. The computer projects the information onto a monitor. Scientists are trying to learn more about the properties of nanoscale objects and how they can be used.

Scientists use a very powerful computer (right) and an extremely sensitive microscope to view tiny nanoscale objects.

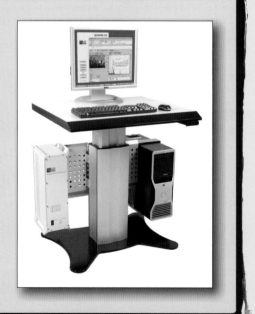

the carpet cloak, there was no shadow. The cloaked bump looked flat. This happened because the cloak reflected light around the bump so that there was no shadow.

More Research Needed

With metamaterials scientists can control and bend light in ways they never thought possible. Still, a lot of research remains. The carpet cloaks made by Zhang and others work in only two dimensions. Because light hits an object from all directions, a useful cloak would have to be 3-dimensional.

The electromagnetic spectrum has many different wavelengths. Scientists will have to research different materials and designs to control light at each wave-

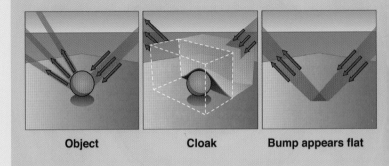

The Carpet Cloak

Object   Cloak   Bump appears flat

length. They will need to shrink metamaterials to work with the shortest light waves. The cloak needs to control many different types of light at the same time. For example, a cloak that only works for yellow light is not very useful.

With more research, the technology to make an object invisible will continue to evolve. The ability to make an object invisible changes the way people "see" the world.

Chapter 4

How Invisibility Cloaks Could Change the World

Scientists are working to make useful invisibility cloaks. They hope to make a cloak that works in a wide range of light. The possible uses for the cloaks are exciting. The military wants to use cloaking to protect soldiers and equipment. Scientists think cloaks could also be used outside of the military. Invisibility cloaks may improve health care and protect against natural disasters. They may also improve any technology that uses light waves.

An invisibility cloak covers every part of this man's body but his hands. It appears that the truck in front of him is visible through the cloak.

Changing War and Law Enforcement

Invisibility cloaks may change how armies fight wars. Invisible armies and equipment would have the advantage of surprise. They would also be safer because they could not be seen.

In addition to the military, police departments could use invisibility cloaks in many ways. An invisible officer could stake out a suspect without being seen. Cloaked SWAT teams would have the advantage of surprise when they entered a building.

Improving Health Care

Invisibility cloaks may one day help doctors and surgeons. When repairing tiny holes in blood vessels or organs, sometimes surgeons' own hands and instruments block

A special image of an "invisible" soldier shows how invisibility technology may be used in the future.

? Did You Know?

Scientists may use invisibility technology to control sound waves. With this ability they could create a quiet spot in the middle of a noisy room.

Shrinking Cell Phones

Scientists can design metamaterials that work with radio waves, radar, and telecommunications signals. Small metamaterials antennas could work as well as larger antennas to receive and send signals. With them, engineers could shrink cell phone antennas. That would lead to smaller phones and wireless devices. They could also be used in many new wireless devices that need many small antennas that work across different bands of signals.

their view. A surgeon could solve this problem by wearing an invisibility glove or cloaking his or her instruments. The surgeon's hands and instruments would become invisible. Then the surgeon could see the surgery site without anything getting in the way. Surgeons could also cloak the patient's bones and organs. This would give them direct sight to the organs and tissues underneath.

Cloaking could also help doctors when using magnetic resonance imaging (MRI). MRI machines use a magnetic field and radio waves to create images of organs and tissues in the body. Because MRI machines have a magnetic field, they sometimes disrupt sensitive medical devices. These devices could be shielded with a cloak. The MRI waves would flow around them as if they were not there.

Protecting from Natural Disasters

Cloaking may protect people and buildings during a natural disaster. Scientists may be able to create metamaterials that work on different types of waves. An earthquake

Did You Know?

Scientists hope metamaterials can one day make a cloak that would redirect something solid. It would be the ultimate bullet-proof vest.

Improving the View

Cloaking technology may help people see more in the future. Projecting an image of the ground on a plane's floor would turn it into a flying glass-bottom boat. Cloaking parts of cars would eliminate blind spots for drivers. People could look through cloaked walls as if they were windows. City planners could cloak an ugly factory building to open up sweeping views of a lake behind it. One day invisibility cloaks may do more than make things disappear. They may open up entire new areas to be seen.

Cloaking parts of a car, such as the divider between the front and rear windows, could remove one of the driver's blind spots.

This shield could protect a house from earthquakes, since a quake's "waves" would flow around it.

The science of metamaterials could also be used in other types of cloaks. Special cloaks could control water waves. They could protect oil rigs and coastlines from sudden storms or **tsunamis**.

Bringing Objects into Focus

Invisibility cloaks make objects disappear. But the science behind them may soon bring the tiniest objects into sight. Scientists are working on a hyperlens, a very powerful lens that is made of metamaterials. A lens is usually made of glass and can change the direction of light waves. Microscopes and cameras use lenses to focus light. This allows researchers to see tiny objects. Today there are limits to what scientists can see with microscopes and magnifying lenses. A living cell that

releases **seismic** waves. Surface seismic waves travel across the earth's surface. They cause the most damage during an earthquake. Scientists think that an earthquake cloak could be built into a building's foundation. When an earthquake strikes, its seismic waves would bend around the building. The building and the people inside would be untouched.

In the Wrong Hands

Invisibility technology could improve life in many ways. Still, some people worry that it could be used in the wrong way. Some people think that the government could use invisible agents to spy on citizens. Others fear that criminals will use invisibility cloaks to commit crimes unseen. Speeders may try radar-absorbing paint on their cars to escape police radar. In the wrong hands, it is possible that invisibility cloaks could become very dangerous.

is magnified 100,000 times may be blurry. Its finest details still cannot be seen.

To make an object invisible, metamaterials reflect light away. To make a tiny object more visible, they could instead concentrate light. They could also gather up light missed by normal lenses. Lenses made with metamaterials may be able to create very fine beams of light. This may allow scientists to see objects that are as small as the wavelength of visible light.

This supermicroscope could make scientific research easier.

People around the world have dreamed of invisibility cloaks. Invisibility, however, is just the beginning. Cloaking science can improve every device that uses electromagnetic waves. Cell phones, antennas, radar, and microscopes could be made smaller, faster, and better. The science of invisibility cloaks may change what humans can see or not see in the years to come.

Glossary

aerodynamic [air-oh-die-NAM-ik]: Designed to move through the air easily and quickly.

animation [an-uh-MAY-shun]: A series of cartoonlike drawings that appear to be in motion when made into movies or videos.

densities [DEN-sit-eez]: How heavy or light objects are for their size. Density is measured by dividing an object's weight by its volume.

electromagnetic [uh-lek-tro-mag-NET-ik]: Energy carried by electric and magnetic waves.

geometric [jee-uh-MEH-trik]: Relating to a branch of mathematics that deals with lines, angles, surfaces, and solid shapes.

infrared [IN-fra-red]: Light that is just longer than red in the visible spectrum and has wavelengths between 750 nanometers and 1 millimeter.

magnesium fluoride [mag-NEEZ-ee-um FLOOR-ide]: A white crystalline salt.

manipulating [man-IP-you-late-ing]: Moving or controlling in a skillful manner.

microwaves [MIKE-roh-waves]: Electromagnetic waves that can pass through solid objects. Microwaves are used in radar.

mirages [muh-RAZH-iz]: Visual effects that create the illusion of a pool of water in which distant objects are reflected upside down. The effects are caused by the bending of light rays and is sometimes seen at sea, in the desert, or when light passes through a prism.

nanometers [NAN-oh-meet-urs]: Units of measurement that are one-billionth of a meter.

nanoscale [NAN-oh-skale]: Something that is measured in nanometers.

optical [OP-tik-uhl]: Designed to aid sight. Having to do with eyes or eyesight.

perpendicular [perp-in-DIK-you-luhr]: At right (90-degree) angles to a line or surface.

refraction [re-FRAK-shun]: The bending of a ray of light when it passes from one substance into another.

seismic [SIZE-mik]: Caused by an earthquake or vibration of the earth.

silicon [SIL-uh-kon]: A nonmetallic element that is found in the earth's crust. It is used in making glass, concrete, brick, pottery, and semiconducting materials.

silicone [SIL-uh-kohn]: A human-made compound that can be liquid, solid, or gel in form. It is heat resistant and can be rubberlike.

stealth [stelth]: An action that is intended not to attract attention.

terrain [ter-RAYN]: The features of an area of land.

texture [TEXT-yur]: A rough or grainy surface quality.

tsunamis [soo-NAH-meez]: Huge waves caused by an undersea earthquake or volcanic eruption.

For More Information

DVDs

That's Impossible: Invisibility Cloaks. Directed by John Ealer. The History Channel, 2009. This 50-minute show reviews the history of invisibility, looks at the latest scientific breakthroughs, and features a demonstration of an invisibility cloak.

Web Sites to Visit

Exploring the Science of Light (www .optics4kids.com). This Web site is sponsored by the Optical Society of America. It features biographies, time lines, tutorials, images, and reference materials.

Physics4Kids (www.physics4kids. com/index.html). This Web site gives information on a variety of physics topics, including light, electricity, and magnetism.

Science News for Kids (www.science newsforkids.org). This Web site is devoted to science news for children. It offers articles about the latest scientific developments as well as suggestions for activities, books, articles, and related Web sites.

Index

A
Aircraft
  radar tracking of, 17
  stealth, 18–20
Alexandria (Egypt), 11
Athena (Greek goddess), 7

B
B-2 bomber, 19
Blue-screen/green-screen backgrounds, 10–11
Brosnan, Pierce, 23
Bulletproof vests, 41

C
Camouflage, 6–7
  of Alexandria, Egypt, 11
  dazzle, 8
  military's use of, 7–8, 10–11, 13–14
  optical, 11–12
  origin of word, 13

Carpet cloak, 35–37
Cars, 41
Cell phones, 40
Chase, Chevy, 22
Churchill, Winston, 11

D
Dazzle camouflage, 8

E
Earthquake cloaks, 41–42
Electromagnetic spectrum, 27, 37

F
F-117 aircraft, 17
Forrest Gump (film), 23

G
Goldenrod spider, 15

H
Harry Potter, 4–5

Harry Potter and the Sorcerer's Stone (film), 22
Health care, 39–40
The Hobbit (Tolkien), 24
Hopeless Diamond, 19

I
Infrared light, 34
Invisibility cloaks, 12, 13
  building with metamaterials, 32–33
  effects on vision of wearer, 34
  impact on health care, 39–40
  impact on military/law enforcement, 39
Invisibility/invisibility technology
  benefits of, 5–6
  in fiction, 24

by manipulation of light, 25
  misuse of, 43
The Invisible Man (Wells), 24

L
Law enforcement, 39
Light
  characteristics of, 26
  color of, 27
  controlling, 28–30
  infrared, 34
  reflection/refraction of, 27–28
  wavelengths of, 26–30, 32, 37
Lockheed Corporation, 19

M
Magnetic resonance imaging (MRI), 40
Maskelyne, Jasper, 11

About the Author

Carla Mooney is the author of several books for young adults and children. She lives in Pittsburgh, Pennsylvania, with her husband and three children.